In Love

Visions of Expanding Love

Also by Stephen C. Paul, with paintings
by Gary Max Collins

ILLUMINATIONS

INNERACTIONS

In Love

*Visions of
Expanding Love*

STEPHEN C. PAUL, Ph.D.

with paintings by

GARY MAX COLLINS

HarperSanFrancisco
A Division of HarperCollins*Publishers*

FIRST EDITION

LIBRARY OF CONGRESS CATALOGING-IN-PUBLICATION DATA
Paul, Stephen C.
    In Love: visions of expanding love / Stephen C. Paul ; with
paintings by Gary Max Collins.
        p.   cm.
    ISBN 0-06-251127-0 (pbk.)
    1. Love—Quotations, maxims, etc.   I. Collins, Gary, 1936-   .
II. Title.
PN6084.L6P38   1995
818′ .5402–dc20   94-7989
                                                           CIP

95 96 97 98 99 ❖ HCP-HK 10 9 8 7 6 5 4 3 2 1

This edition is printed on acid-free paper that meets the American
National Standards Institute Z39.48 Standard.

This book

is dedicated

to those

who open.

Introduction

In our first book, *Illuminations,* we challenge you to drop your protective mask, face your fears, and express yourself honestly, directly, and fully. In *Inneractions,* we ask you to live life out of a new, fresh perspective originating inside yourself and to take the necessary steps to bring the outside world into harmony with that internal vision. Meeting those challenges creates an inner and an outer peace that sets the stage for the ultimate adventure.

In Love invites you to open to love. The book begins with the love you must have for yourself and then spirals outward to embrace intimate relationships, relationships in the larger world around you, and ultimately the divine. The message is simple. It is possible to love and be loved. It is essential.

Allow Gary's oil images to draw your attention, relax and soften you. Let these words and images combine to open your heart.

Start with yourself

and let your love

grow outward

in ever-expanding circles.

You long

to be loved

and long

to give love.

You will find love here

because you're here

to find

and to bring love.

You are always in relationship,

whether you realize it or not,

so the only question is

whether you are consciously relating.

No matter where you are

or what your circumstances

it is always possible

to experience boundless love.

Only your own

sense of separateness

can keep you

feeling apart.

If you are afraid

to open to love,

it is only because

you're so very tender.

Spend time alone

and discover

your most constant

and cherished companion.

Take a fresh look

and see yourself

without the distortions

of others' perceptions.

You are not

your fears or defenses

but what lies protected

behind them.

You must first

accept your limitations

before you will ever

accept your love.

Love yourself enough

to always express

your true feelings,

needs, and limits.

Bring every aspect of your life

fully in line with your integrity.

Include yourself

in every situation

by being

fully present.

Opening to feel love

and to express love

in any of countless ways

gives your life meaning.

You are never

so beautiful

as when

your heart opens.

In those moments when

self-consciousness recedes

and your heart opens,

there is only love.

Love yourself

as a

unique expression

of everything divine.

Love is the energy

that flows in a circle

between you and another

when you both open.

Relationship is not the drama

of pursuing unobtainable love

but loving and being loved

where it is obtainable.

Pick your path

and then

pick a companion

on the same journey.

When you invite

love to come,

never settle for less

than the love you desire.

If you give yourself up

for another's love,

your gift of sacrifice

will include your resentment.

Only open to love

with someone who wants to

respect and protect

your personal boundaries.

The flow of your love

is broken

by unexpressed

anger and pain.

All words thrown

across a gulf

of separateness

will sting like stones.

Once you withdraw your energy,

you will be gone even if you stay.

There is nothing

more painful

than being alone

together.

In order to love completely

you must stay present

despite

the urge to withdraw.

To be present,

release the past and the future,

focus on the moment,

and open your heart.

Become aware of how you

extend and withdraw

your life energy

in response to others.

Be certain

you are open

before you

express yourself.

Love can

abide only

where the truth

is spoken.

Love your partner enough

to tell the truth,

and love yourself enough

to demand it.

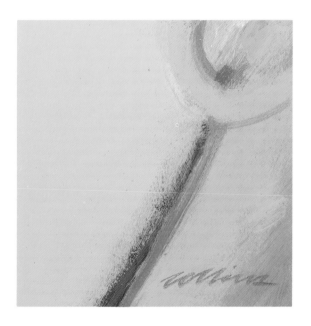

You can

feel love

and any other feeling

at the same time.

To have what you want in relationship

you must each commit

to press beyond your personal limits

and to support each other's changes.

Gently show each other

the limits of your loving

so you can learn together

to love beyond them.

Relate to your partner

rather than

to your assumptions

about your partner.

Attachment

always

turns love

into something less.

You are attached

if another's life

becomes more about you

than it is about him or her.

Those you love

are free

to stay or go

and to choose what they would give.

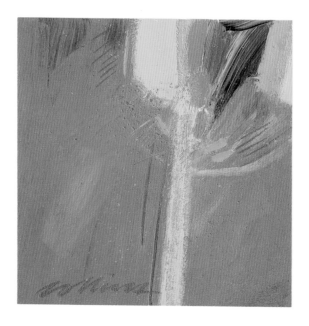

Feel your love

and let that feeling

give rise to

the expressions of your love.

Each time

you touch your lover,

touch him or her

with your love.

It becomes natural

to relax, laugh, and play

once you heal the issues

that block the flow of love.

It's a delight

to travel through life

with a companion

who becomes a true friend.

When your need for love

is already filled inside your relationship,

you can carry your love together

into the world.

Love is a feeling of fullness

that grows inside

until it overflows

and must be given away.

You are free to love

only after

you are free

to trust.

Approach everyone you meet

as though he or she were

hurt, afraid,

and tender like you.

To know a person,

be with him or her alone,

outside

your usual roles.

You can

know another

only to the extent

that he or she guides your way.

If you

are to love here,

your love must

embrace limitations.

When your heart is open,

compassion is

the only point of view

and the only course of action.

You will never

feel loved

unless you accept

love when it's offered.

Recognize that

within their limitations

people are continually

offering you love.

The goal is not

to act in loving ways

but to feel your love

and to let it guide your actions.

Show respect for

anyone you meet

by being

fully present.

Always acknowledge

the precious gift

someone gives

by opening to you.

It takes so very little

to acknowledge

that you recognize

someone else's value.

People will melt

at the touch

of your

recognition.

Thank those

who offer you their love,

and tell them often

how very much you care.

Each time you reveal your love

to another person,

you remind that person

of the love in his or her own heart.

Every time you touch someone

with your open heart,

it sends a healing ripple

farther than you'll ever know.

When you are open

with another,

you experience

the presence of God.

Love is

the substance

beneath the illusion

in every creation.

Don't mistake your limited perception of love

for the unlimited nature of love.

In nature,

you experience

the perfect expression of spirit

in physical form.

The flowers and the asphalt,

the forests and the power lines

are equally part

of everything divine.

Nature offers you

the perfect example

of continually changing

unconditional love.

The frightening, the ugly,

and the heartbreaking

that you encounter in the world

reveal the remnants of your judgments.

Rather than reject

harsh realities,

accept them as a part of

all that you're here to experience.

It takes great courage

to see harshness

and pain

and still stay open.

You're always living

in life's illusion

and in love

at the same time.

You are not separate

from anyone or anything—

despite

all appearances.

Look past the differences

that separate people

and see the human beings

that are within.

Behind all appearances,

there is always

something more

for you to see.

You are different than,

very similar to,

and the same as

everything you see.

Dissolve the illusion

of separation

between yourself

and all that you encounter.

There is love

and there is everything else

and both must be addressed

in every interaction.

In nature,

separateness falls away

and you remember

your place in the mystery.

When you connect

with nature,

you connect with

the expansive part of yourself.

Take time

to be with the earth

and you will remember

how very much you love her.

Be alone

with the earth

and you will hear God

sing you love songs.

Everything

on this planet

will be touched

by your notice.

If you first love the earth

with all of your heart,

your loving actions

will naturally follow.

The act of creation

is to love something

that does not yet exist

into existence.

Love is

moving

in harmony

with the universe.

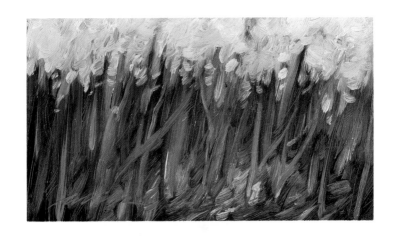

You are part of

an ever-expanding,

ever-developing,

and always loving consciousness.

You are

consciousness

recognizing

itself.

Don't be afraid.

You're always embraced

in the arms

of the universe.

Speak your heart

and be willing

to listen

for the ever-present answer.

Soften, relax,

and open

to the love

that surrounds you.

Devotion is

when your heart

bursts

with your love.

When you open,

the love of the universe

is free

to pass through you.

The sensation

when your heart

opens to love

is ecstasy.

You are

already loved

beyond your ability

to imagine.

You will be in the midst

of the greatest joy

as you become a part

of everything.

Acknowledgments

Gary and I are very grateful to family members, partners, friends, and colleagues who have helped us to realize just how important love is in our lives. We would both like to thank Barbara Moulton, our editor at Harper San Francisco, for her encouragement and contributions to this book. My clients have shared the trials, glories, and lessons of their relationships with me. I am deeply appreciative. I must thank Jackie. She has helped me shape this book. More importantly, she has helped turn it into a reality in my life.

About the Author

Stephen C. Paul, Ph.D., is a psychotherapist, educator, artist, and Tai Chi instructor based in Salt Lake City, Utah. He received his doctorate in clinical psychology from the University of Missouri and has taught and counseled at the University of Utah. His private practice focuses on brief, intensive work with people who are highly motivated to change.

About the Artist

Gary Collins's paintings are exhibited internationally. A native of Utah, he has been painting as far back as he can remember, with marked success since 1972. Before that he was a successful designer, businessman, and consultant. His crowning achievement, he says, is that his daughter and son are both successful artists as well.